Keeping Me Healthy

My Body and What it Needs

by Ruth Owen

Ruby Tuesday Books

Published in 2016 by Ruby Tuesday Books Ltd.

Editor: Mark J. Sachner
Designer: Emma Randall
Consultant: Judy Wearing, PhD, BEd
Production: John Lingham

Photo credits:
Alamy: 7 (bottom), 22 (bottom left); Getty Images: 22 (bottom right); Shutterstock: Cover, 1, 2–3, 4–5, 6, 7 (top), 8–9, 10–11, 12–13, 14–15, 16–17, 18–19, 20–21, 22 (top), 23, 24–25, 26–27, 28–29, 30–31.

British Library Cataloguing in Publication Data (CIP) is available for this title.

ISBN 978-1-910549-84-1

Printed in Poland by L&C Printing Group

www.rubytuesdaybooks.com

Contents

Words shown in **bold** in the text are explained in the glossary.

The download button shows there are free worksheets or other resources available. Go to:

www.rubytuesdaybooks.com/scienceKS1

All About Your Body

Every day you think, talk, eat, move and have fun. This is all possible because of your amazing body.

So how does your body work? And what does it need?

Get ready to think like a scientist and discover lots about YOU!

Ear

Cheek

Eye

Nose

Mouth

Chin

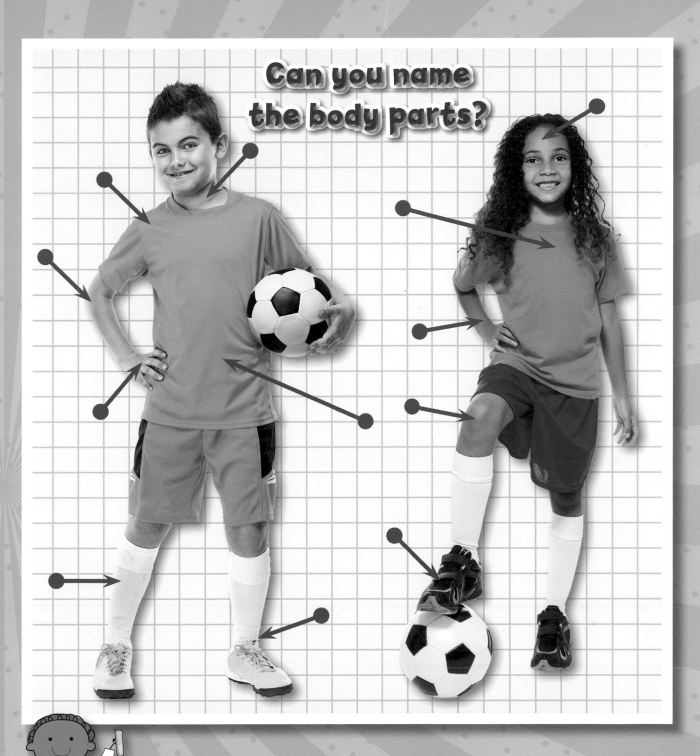

Can you name the body parts?

Be a Scientist!

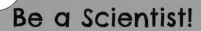

Look at these words for body parts.

Can you match the words to the picture above?

Neck	Shoulder	Knee
Arm	Chest	Ankle
Elbow	Belly	Foot
Head	Hand	Leg

Choose five of the body parts. Then in a notebook, write a sentence about that body part. For example:

I kick a football with my foot.

Let's Look Inside

Inside your body is a strong framework of bones called a skeleton.

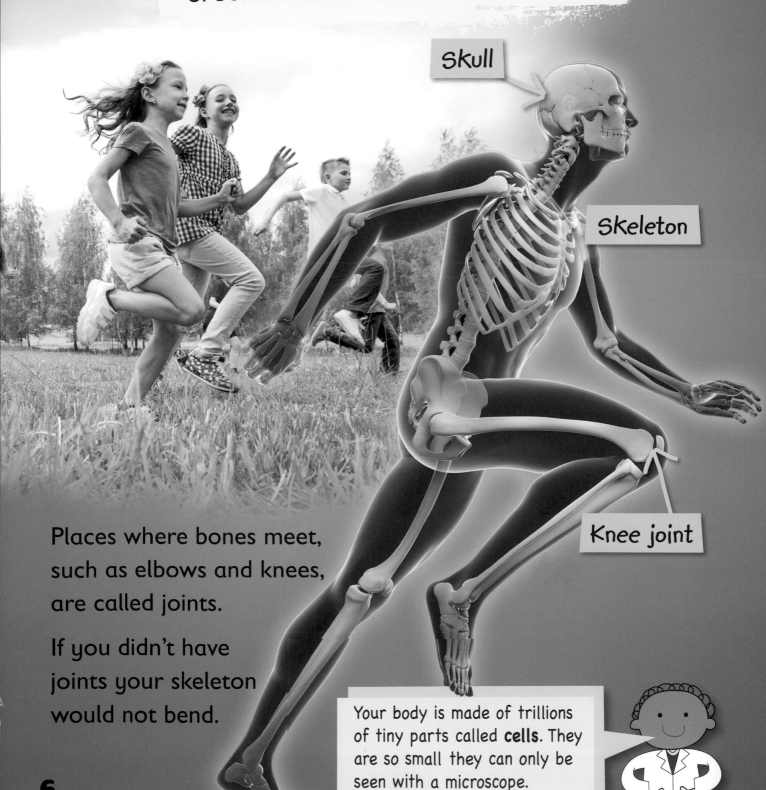

Skull

Skeleton

Knee joint

Places where bones meet, such as elbows and knees, are called joints.

If you didn't have joints your skeleton would not bend.

Your body is made of trillions of tiny parts called **cells**. They are so small they can only be seen with a microscope.

You have hundreds of muscles in your body. Their job is to move your bones.

Your muscles are attached to your bones by stretchy, cord-like tendons.

Let's Investigate!

Gently examine your fingers.

Can you feel the hard bones inside?

How many joints does each finger have?

Now look at the back of your hand and wriggle your fingers. Muscles in your hand and arm are moving the finger bones.

Can you see the cord-like tendons that attach the muscles to the finger bones?

Where do you see them moving?

(There are answers at the bottom of the page.)

If you could *see* inside your hand, this is what you would see.

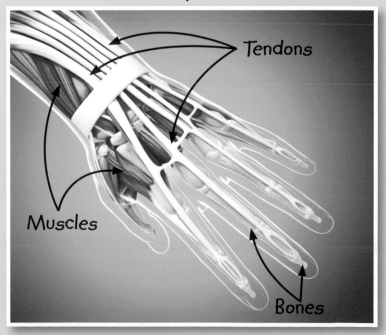

Tendons

Muscles

Bones

Answers: You have three bones and three joints in each finger. When you wriggle your fingers you'll see the tendons moving on the back of your hand and up your arm.

7

Your Brain in Charge

Safe inside your hard, bony skull is your brain. This **organ** is your body's control centre.

Day and night, it's hard at work sending instructions...

...when you're swimming...

...smiling and laughing...

...choosing what book to read...

...eating and drinking...

Your brain controls actions such as breathing and blinking. Your body does these things without you having to think about them.

...turning cartwheels.

9

Your Heart and Blood

To keep working your body needs **oxygen** from the air. It also needs water and **nutrients** from your food.

Your blood delivers all these things to cells around your body.

It's your heart's job to pump, or push, your blood around your body.

Blood vessels

Heart

Your blood travels through thousands of kilometres of tiny tubes called blood vessels.

What Is Blood Made Of?

The main ingredient in your blood is a watery liquid called plasma.

Your blood also contains red blood cells and white blood cells.

Inside a blood vessel

Red blood cells

White blood cells

Your white blood cells attack germs and help you fight illnesses.

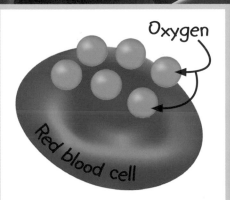

Oxygen

Red blood cell

Red blood cells deliver oxygen to cells that need it.

Breathing In and Out

Your muscles and other body parts need oxygen to produce **energy**. When you breathe in you take oxygen into your lungs.

Oxygen

Your blood collects oxygen from your lungs and delivers it around your body.

As it produces energy your body makes **carbon dioxide.**

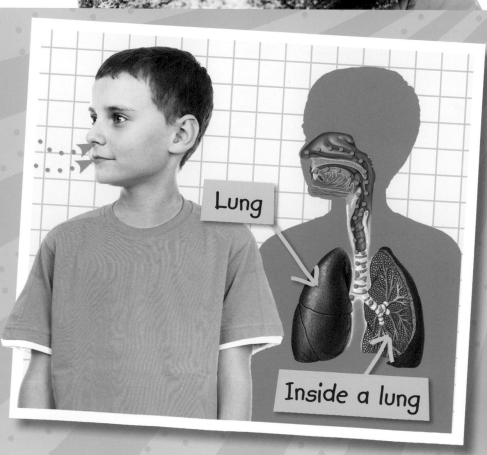

Lung

Inside a lung

Your body doesn't need carbon dioxide so your blood collects it.

Then it carries the unwanted gas back to your lungs and you breathe it out.

Why do you puff when you run? It's because your brain tells you to breathe in more and more oxygen so your body can produce energy.

You and Your Food

To grow and be healthy your body needs nutrients. You get nutrients from food and drink.

You swallow food and drink and it goes down into your stomach.

Your teeth chew the food.

Juices in your stomach turn the food into a gloopy mixture like a smoothie.

From your stomach the food mixture
moves into your small intestine.

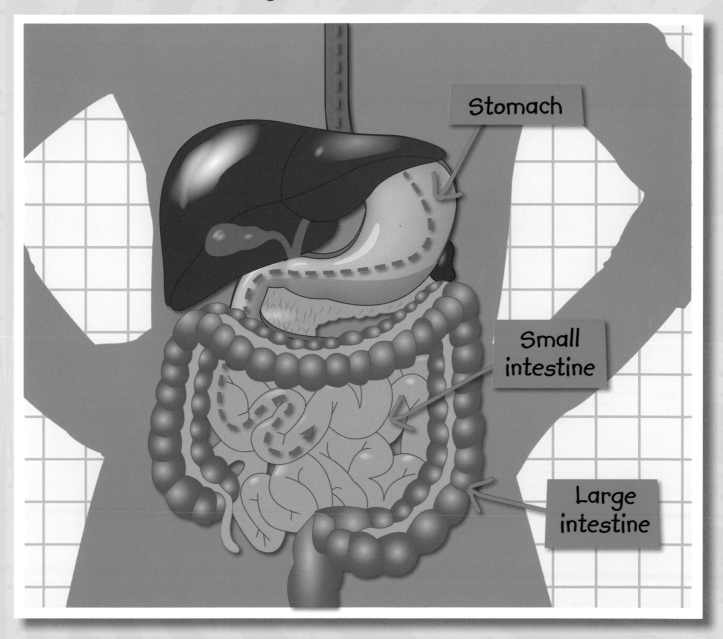

Stomach

Small
intestine

Large
intestine

In your small intestine water and nutrients from your
food are released into your blood.

There are lots of different
nutrients in your food.
The main ones include
carbohydrates, protein, fat,
vitamins and **minerals**.

The material then moves
through your large intestine.

The leftovers leave your
body as poo.

Wonderful Water

To keep your body happy and healthy you should drink plenty of water.

How Much Should I Drink Each Day?

Try to drink six to eight glasses of water and other liquids such as milk or fruit juice.

100% fruit juice no added sugar

Fruit juice

Milk

80% water

Some fruits and vegetables contain lots of water.

90% water

To work properly, the cells in your body need water.

Your body also needs water
to make your blood.

As blood travels around your body
it picks up unwanted substances.
Some of this waste leaves your
body in your wee. Your body uses
water to make wee.

Let's Talk

How does your body tell
you that it needs a drink?
(The answer is at the bottom of the page.)

Answer: The feeling of being thirsty is your body's way of telling you it needs water.
So get a drink of water and NEVER ignore this feeling.

Let's Eat!

To be healthy we should eat lots of different foods each day.

The food we eat can be sorted into four main groups.

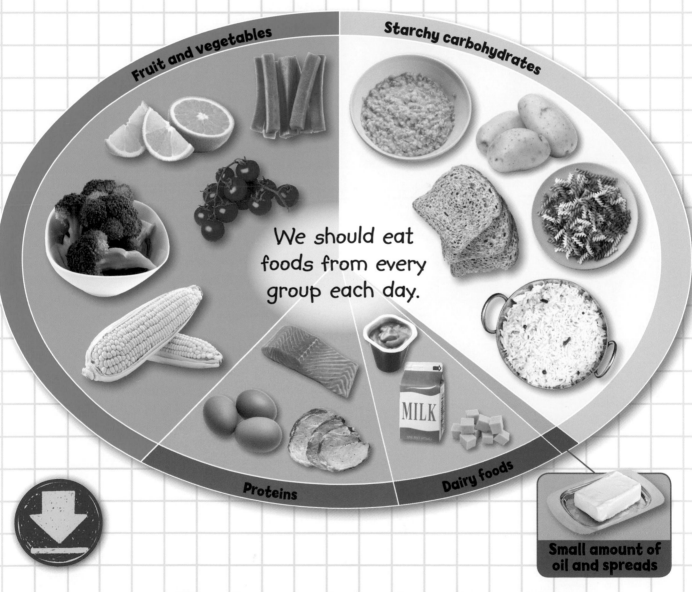

Fruit and vegetables

Starchy carbohydrates

We should eat foods from every group each day.

Proteins

Dairy foods

Small amount of oil and spreads

MILK

The diagram shows that we should eat lots of fruit, vegetables and carbohydrates.

We need to eat smaller amounts of proteins and dairy foods.

Carbohydrate Foods

- Give us energy to stay active.
- Give us fibre to keep our stomachs and intestines healthy.

Pasta

Couscous

Potatoes

Wraps

Bread

Cereal

Protein Foods

- Help our bodies to grow and make repairs.
- Give us energy.
- Give us healthy skin.
- Keep our brains healthy.

Eggs

Meat

Peanut butter

Tuna fish

Beans

Dairy Foods

- Contain calcium for healthy bones and teeth.
- Give us protein and vitamins.
- Keep our brains healthy.
- Give us energy.
- Give us healthy skin.

Milk

Cheese

Fromage frais

Sugary, fatty foods, such as sweets and biscuits, should only be eaten now and again in small amounts. They can make us overweight and sugar can damage our teeth.

Chocolate

Biscuits

Five a Day

Fruit and vegetables are very good for us. We should eat at least five portions of these foods every day.

Each of the pictures shows a portion.

Mixed berries

Strawberries

Peas

Sweetcorn

Broccoli

Banana

Stir-fried vegetables

Vegetable kebab

Let's Explore

Choose five different portions from the pictures. Make sure you include some fruit and some vegetables.

Why did you choose these five?

When will you eat your five a day?

Breakfast Lunch Dinner Snacks

Plan a menu for a day.

What other foods will you eat with your fruits and vegetables? Make sure you include carbohydrates, dairy foods and proteins.

Apple

Cherry tomatoes

Salad

Cucumber

Carrots and beans

Satsumas

Grapes

Fruit and Vegetables

- Give us lots of vitamins.
- Help our bodies fight off illnesses.
- Give us energy.
- Give us fibre which is good for our stomachs and intestines.

Let's Go!

It's great fun to be active and it's good for your body, too. There are lots of different ways to get exercise every day!

Go for a walk.

Visit a playground.

Play a sport.

22

Go for a bike ride.

Let's Invent It!

Can you invent a game to play outdoors?

Your new game must include lots of activity such as running or jumping. Think about some ideas:

Will your game be for one person, two people or more?

Do you need equipment such as a ball?

Do the players become characters such as superheroes or pirates?

What are the rules for your game and what is it called?

Let's play!

23

Happy, Healthy Skin

Your skin is your body's protective covering. It stops dirt and germs getting into your body.

Have a bath or shower regularly to keep your skin clean and healthy.

SPF 50
Sunscreen

Sunshine is good for you but the Sun's light can hurt your skin.
So protect your skin with sunscreen.

Washing your hands with soap and water stops germs spreading.

1. Wet your hands with clean water.

2. Turn off the tap and apply soap.

3. Rub and scrub your hands for 20 seconds.

4. Rinse your hands with clean water.

5. Dry your hands.

You can use a brush to scrub under your nails.

When should I wash my hands?

Before touching food.

After playing outside.

After going to the toilet.

After blowing my nose.

After touching pets.

Time to Brush

Have you had any wobbly teeth yet? When one of your baby teeth falls out, a new tooth grows.

By the time you are a teenager your 28 permanent teeth will have replaced your baby teeth.

Take good care of these new teeth, because they must last for your whole life!

Your teeth are the hardest part of your body. They are even harder than your bones.

Brush your teeth for two minutes at least twice a day.

One time should be just before you go to bed.

Let's Test It

When you brush your teeth can you estimate how long two minutes is?

Ask a helper to time you using a watch or phone.

Start brushing your teeth.

When you think two minutes have passed stop brushing.

How close did you get to two minutes?

Next time you brush try timing yourself using a watch or phone.

Let's Talk

What do you do every night that is very good for your body?

Time for Bed

It might seem like going to bed is a waste of time but it's not!

As you sleep, your busy brain, muscles and other body parts get a chance to rest.

When you are seven to 12 years old, your body needs up to 11 hours of sleep each night.

During the day your heart beats about 80 times each minute.

When you are asleep it slows down a little.

Resting at night helps to keep your heart healthy.

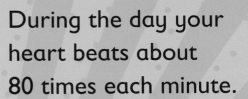

Your skin is busy healing cuts and scrapes and your bones and muscles grow.

Get Ready for Tomorrow!

After a good night's sleep you'll be ready to do your schoolwork.

It will be easier for you to remember what you learn, too.

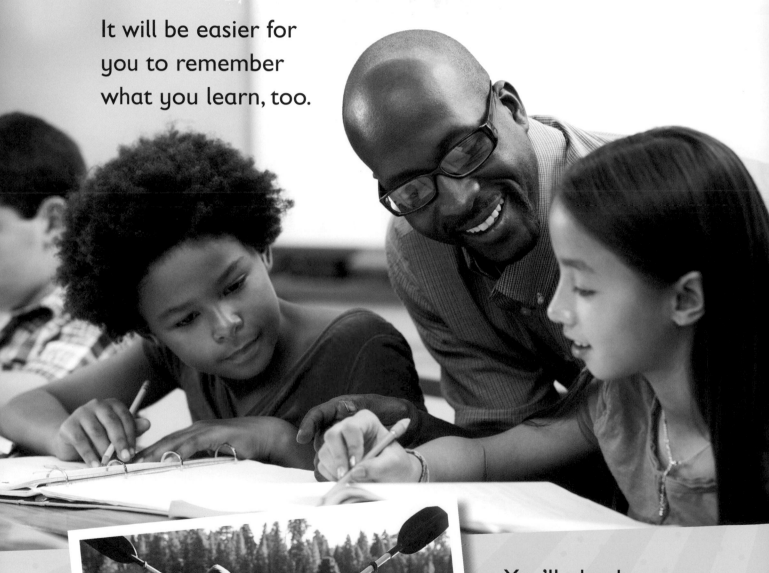

You'll also have lots of energy for sport, playing and other activities.

When it's time for bed settle down for a good sleep.

Try to go to bed at the same time each night. Your body will get used to the routine and it will know it's time to sleep.

Don't have a TV or computer near your bed. The bright lights can make your body think it's daytime. This stops you falling asleep.

Make sure your bedroom is quiet and dark.

When morning comes you'll feel happy, healthy and energised!

Glossary

carbon dioxide
An invisible gas in the air. People and animals breathe out this gas.

cells
Very tiny parts of a living thing. Your bones, skin, hair and every part of you are made of cells.

energy
The ability to do work or be active.

mineral
A kind of nutrient in food important for the body's health and growth, such as calcium or iron.

nutrient
A substance, such as a vitamin or mineral, that a living thing needs to grow and be healthy.

organ
A body part, such as the brain or heart, that has a particular job to do.

oxygen
An invisible gas in air and water that most living things need for survival.

vitamin
A kind of nutrient in food important for the body's health and growth, such as vitamin C or vitamin A.

Index